Dear Baby

Matters of the Heart

Curtis Givens

ISBN: 978-0-578-15892-1

Facebook:
https://www.facebook.com/CurtisGivens
https://www.facebook.com/dearbabypoetry

Twitter:
https://twitter.com/Givens1

Pinterest:
https://www.pinterest.com/curtisgivens/~dear-baby~/

Website:
http://dearbabygivens1.wix.com/dearbaby

❧Dedication☙

I dedicate my life and this book to my children Boogy, Button, Mounkah, Gouda, and Todah.

To my mother, Lettie Ruise, you are my heart and strength. I appreciate you.

To my father, Randy J. Givens III, know that you are dear to me.

❧In Loving Memory❧
Your Presence Is Still Felt

Roosevelt (Bug) Smith Jr

❧Acknowledgements❧

As I continue to write, express, and feel, I welcome people to come and share this ride of pure bliss.

I want give honor to My Lord and Savior Jesus Christ for granting me this gift for writing and allowing me to meet and bless those I've come in contact. I pray, as I continue to write, he will allow me to grow, and guide me allowing my words to give him glory.

For guidance and words of astonishing insight, I would like to thank Monica Convington Doris Marie Barner, Ms.Runae Stiles, Leslie Stevens, Sonja Ranea Armstrong, Lorenzo Marc Williams, LaQuisha Tashawn Bridges, Natasha Davis, Sonja Larkin, Brotha Heru Ra Kemet, Edsel Peterson, Mitzi Smith, Juanita Hughes, Dawn Warren, Chris Cook, Kimberly Bowman, Rodney Frazier and a host of other friends and family who has supported me, as well as encouraged me to follow my dreams.

✍What Is Love?✍

1 Corinthians 13:4- 8 NIV (4) Love is patient, love is kind. It does not envy, it does not boast, it is not proud. (5) It does not dishonor others, it is not self-seeking, it is not easily angered, it keeps no record of wrongs. (6) Love does not delight in evil but rejoices with the truth. (7) It always protects, always trusts, always hopes, always perseveres. (8) Love never fails....

Romans 12:9 NIV (9) Love must be sincere.....

1 John 4:18 NIV (18) There is no fear in love. But perfect love drives out fear.....

1 Peter 4:8 NIV (8) Above all, love each other deeply, because love covers over a multitude of sins.

1 Corinthians 13:13 NIV (13) And now these three remain: faith, hope and love. But the greatest of these is love.

Romans 13:10 NIV (10) Love does no harm to a neighbor. Therefore, Love Is The Fulfillment of The Law.

❧Table of Contents❧

Dear Baby,

It's 2:40am and my thoughts are of you. From the very moment you came into my life, you made my heart happy. My thoughts are focused and my soul is pleased. You brought with you love for me. You came to me with smiles and joy. You showed up to my life with peace. How can one not fall in love with a woman such a beautiful woman like you?

Know that you are to me a Godsend. Know you have my whole heart. Know that for you, I would do anything. Know that you mean the world to me. I love you so very much. Say you'll allow me to love you all the days of your life.

Forever, For Always, For Love,
Curty

๛Make Me Yours๛

When you make me yours,
My domestic experience will be your absolute
bliss.

When you make me yours,
Your happiness is my priority and responsibility.

When you make me yours,
Satisfied would be your answer when asked how
you are?

When you make me your man,
Pleased you will be always.

For your tears will be my tears,
And your smiles, my smiles.

When I'm your man,
You're my one and only love.

Please Baby, make me yours.

❧Adoration❧

To love you is a pleasant effort to partake.
For the value of your heart to me is priceless.
The way I adore you makes my world
worthwhile.
Your smile makes my heart sing songs in ways
that weren't written yet.
Kiss my lips with yours so I can visit heaven
briefly.
Rub my baldhead and ask whatever you want.
My pleasant effort is to love always and I like it.
Kisses to you, My Heart.

∽Learning You∾

I come not only to admire you but also, to
appreciate you in all 360 degrees. Share with me
not only your triumphs but your failures too.
Let's discuss our disagreements respectfully so
that I might gain a new perspective.

What are your aspirations?
What are your hopes?
What are your dreams?
Tell me so that I'm more than aware but, hands
on with helping you achieve them.

Your hard work inspires me.
You're creative, thoughtful, intelligent and that
beautiful mind has driven me to evaluate the
things I wish to accomplish.

On our next date choose a place that helps
channel your moving forward.
On our next encounter, let's talk and discuss
everything. Give me knowledge, Beloved.
I yearn to learn from your experience.
Share with me you and all that you're about.

✄Butterflies✄

When I see your smiling face, I get butterflies in the pit of my soul.

Kiss me with those lips and send warm feelings through my heart.

Baby putting your tiny hands in mine has brought a tear to my eye.

Sometimes, all I need is the air that I breathe and to love you.

Butterflies....damn.

❧For You❧

I can't hold a note to save my life but for I you I'd sing my heart out.

Boiling water is in my range but for you I would turn into Chef Boyardee.

My common colors are bland but for my Queen a wardrobe to die for I would design.

With my hands and your input, a house for you I would build.

Beloved, you deserve heaven. If the Lord allowed me a piece of it, I would give it to you.

Know that from the deepest part of my heart, I love you.

❦Desire❧

How is it that you generate in me such a desire
for a kiss from you? I mean, when you put your
waist in my hands and your fragrance lingers
until it reaches its initial target and when you
stand on your tippy toes with head tilted and
plants on my lips something amazing....what am
I to do?

I'm enchanted by what a simple peck from you
does to me. Your kiss on my lips cures all that
the day brings that is bad. Come, let's steal
away for a moment from prying eyes so that
your lips can bless mine.

One kiss is all I need....
Ok, maybe two.

❧You❧

The way you walk turns me on
When I'm following behind you
When you call my name
Your laugh
When you cry softly
The fragrance you wear
When you cook my favorite meal
The frown you make when you're angry
The way you look before we go to bed
When you read to the kids
The way you feel next to me
When you show me you love me
By having my back
It's the little things

❧Just One Night❧

Baby, don't go into work tonight. Please stay home so I can hold you and have you to myself. Every time you go away, a piece of me goes with you. I miss you and I'm lonely without you.

Please stay home with me tonight because it's cold outside and I need and want you near me. Baby, please call out. Breakfast in bed, I promise, as soon as the sun shines her face. Will you tell your boss you aren't coming in tonight. Please?!?! Just one night....

❧Will We Sleep Tonight❧

Your essence has me captivated to the point of gazing. Let me embrace you with security promised and love guaranteed. Holding you in my arms is a fantasy comes true.

In your eyes, I see the love you hold for me. Be my Angel tonight, the next night, and the night after that. Let me dream the dreams that have you where you are now. Will we sleep tonight, Beloved?

❧As You Slept❧

As you slept,
Last night, I couldn't help but notice you.
How peaceful you looked.

As you lay there next to me,
I wondered what you were dreaming.
Sweet dreams or nightmares?

As you lay, in your quiet slumber,
I kissed your cheek and you smiled.
For no particular reason at all I prayed for us.
You relaxed that much more.

It was then, that no matter what,
At the end of the day,
I would put a smile on your face.

As you slept,
I felt the urged to hold you close.
Therefore, I gently grabbed you,
And spooned with you.

It was then, that no matter what,
I knew with all my heart,
I love you.

✦You Are Home✦

Sleep well in my embrace.
Dream incredible.
My arms are for holding you tight and securing
you always. While the moon rides high and the
stars gleam bright, above in my loving care is
where you should be.

Are you comfortable?
If not, what might I do to please you?
What might I do to celebrate your slumber while
you contour and conform to what makes us one.

Close to you is all I need to be. Your fragrance
has captured my attention and your essence has
me captivated. Sleep well my Queen.

❧Any Other Way❧

I love you and I wouldn't have it any other way.
Whenever I see your beautiful beautiful smile,
my heart melts.

On occasions, I find myself reminiscing on how
much I love you and our engaging encounters—
the sweet smell of your body, the warmth of your
love, and the sound of your heartbeat.

I love you so very much.
I wouldn't have it any other way, My Heart.

❧A Reminder of You❧

As a reminder of you, I took the t-shirt you slept
in last night. I hope you don't mind.

As a reminder of how beautiful you are, I
sprayed some your perfume on my shirt, hands
and neck. I hope you don't mind.

From the day you captured my heart my
thoughts are of you.
Throughout my entire day Beloved, you're all
that I think of.
The very things that make you attractive also
make me adore you.

Your smile is my sunshine.
The kisses you give are my healer.
You still send chills through me with your touch.
Baby Girl, with all of my life, I love you.

Every time we are apart, I miss you madly.
To hear you call my name is as if an Angel
spoke. Whatever it takes to make you happy I
will do. By the way, I'm smelling your shirt as I
write.

❧Questions❧

As time has passed, my affections for you are as
I breathe....
I love us.
I enjoy us.
I relish in the experience that makes us one.
My heart and soul morphs into stronger and
more vibrant me whenever you're in my
thoughts.

Why do you Love me so?
Do I prove my worth to you?
With my ego being my daddy's ego, am I good to
you when you need me to be?
Each time you smile, it reminds me of what a
wonderful woman to whom I'm in love with.

⋖You Love Me⋗

You love me because you told me so.
You love me because you showed me so.
Today you've shown me love beyond my
expectations.
On this day you've blessed me with more the
material gifts and well wishes.
As we speak, I'm in heaven from you expressing
to me how much I mean to you.
You love me because you told me so
You love me because you showed me so
Today I got all that I asked for
Today I was blessed beyond words
Today you made me smile by a simply saying,
"Happy Birthday Curty"
You love me because you told me so
You love because you showed me so
My Heart
My Love
My Heaven's Design

❧You Fit❧

You fit.
Your body in my hands secured snuggly in my
arms.
You fit.
Your lips on my own and mine on yours.
You fit.
You understand my heart, mind, and soul.
You fit.
My appreciation for you and your life
experiences is beyond measure.
Our unusual way of being and our unorthodox
style of relating makes me feel as if we have
danced this dance before.
We Fit.

∽Complete∾

Your decision to love me makes my world the
place I want to be.
The complex way you desire my heart gives me
the will to want to be your man.
I dig your fire, your strength and your appetite
for loving me the way you love me.
Complete is the way I feel when you're near me.
Absolute is the way I feel when you're not, but
on your way.
Blessed is the way I feel because I know you're
mine.
Inside of your heart lies a piece of my heart.
Within your soul lies my love and affection.
In your mind are my whispers and confessions
of how you make me feel.
Your decision to love me makes my world the
place to be.

Dear Baby,

Loving you is easy. Caring for you is never a task. Making you smile is a pleasure. Consoling your heart and soul is an absolute joy. A lifetime with you is heaven...my heaven.

Thank you for allowing me to love the way I love you.

Love Always,
Curty

❧Crush❧

Do you know I still have a crush on you?
Have you any idea that you still give me
butterflies?
From the fragrance you adorn,
To the sexy lace that you parade in;
It hugs your body so right.

Do you know I still have a crush on you?
Do you know the reasons for my crush beloved?
It's your smile.
It's your love for me, from your heart.
It's your kisses.
It's your gentle touch to my head and chest, and
inner thigh.
It's your selflessness.
For that Beloved, my crush will always remain.

⧉Feeling Some Kind of Way⧉

Thoughts of you occupy my more than my mind
and I'm feeling elated. Consider you and me on a
consensual love affair that lasts forever and a
few months' time.

My heart holds you dear; he holds you close and
loves you to the end of the world.

Your voice sends chills to my core, your touch
makes me want you and I love you so very very
much.

⊰Your Presence⊱

I want you to know that I'm so in love with you.
Your love has me intoxicated and on a true
natural high.

My mind is racing with thoughts of you so much
so I can't focus. You give good good love to me to
where I'm drooling just thinking about it.

Your very presence makes everything all right
and I so much adore your sunshine Beloved.
I love you inside and out, and from your head to
your beautiful toes.

I love you.

⤳Epic Proportions⤵

My love for you is on the level of epic proportions and my desire is beyond limits.

You Beloved have touched me in ways that I wasn't prepared for. My heart you entered and found a place deep inside and it feels good.

Your beauty has me in awe. Your conversation has my attention and also has me thinking.

The desire and need and the want I have inside for me for you is more than a feeling. I wanting to feel your body in my hands have my imagination wishing for it to be real. There would be nothing more I'd rather do than to please and satisfy your sexual desires and appetites. Just say yes.

My love for you has found another level and it's of epic proportion. May I show you?

✥1000s Ways I Declare✥

In 1000 ways, I declare my love for you in its entire splendor. The key to my Heart you have tightly in your possession. Know that our song plays smoothly in my mind when I think of you.

My smile is because of you and your desire to love me. It feels so good to love you back, Beloved.

Your essence I still wear as I leave your side this morning. I hope my kiss is enough to sustain you for now until we meet somewhere warm and cozy so I can hold you tight next to my heart. Oh yeah...I love you too.

❧Saying It Plain❧

Saying it plain and with my entire heart, I miss you. Although absence makes the heart grow fonder, my heart is fonder when you're next to me. Wanting you by my side only pains me when you're not.

Making it plain I love you with my entire being. Everything about you woman drives me to be all I can be. When I prayed for someone to share my life with, the Lord over blessed me with you. I can't stop thanking Him.

In plain English, I need you. My joy comes from your beautiful soul. My peace comes from your sweet tender voice.

Simply said, I love you.

❧Eternally Yours❧

I love you with every beat of my heart.
I need you with everything I love.
I want you with all that I am.
Eternally Yours

❧Do You Need Me❧

Do you need me? If so, why?
Am I supportive of you and your goals?
Do I challenge you to strive for excellence?
In return, do I accept all that you offer me good
and or otherwise?

Do you need me?
Am I that man that you need and require so that
you are complete?
Baby, my reason for being in your life is God
arranged.
I pray to him that I do right by you and then I
ask you are you happy.

Do you need me Baby...still?
I love you like there is no tomorrow,
For you are my love and my heaven's design.

❧Why Me❧

Why me?
Is it my lips that turn you and your lips on?

Why me?
Why do you love the way my heart loves you?

Why me?
You say you feel safe in my arms....why?
Giving me your smile, your attention, your love
and affection.....why?

Baby please forgive if I'm being ungrateful.
Baby please forgive if I'm trippin.
I ask these questions because I look at how
beautiful, smart and wonderful you are and
wonder to myself why did she give me her *REAL*
phone number?

❧Walk With Me☙

Take my hand and walk with me.
For as long as I'm allowed,
Close to you is where I want to be.
Give me all of you.
I give you all of me.
No limits or restrictions;
Forgive me my weaknesses.

While I'm being strong enough for all of us.
Take my hand and walk with me.
Listen to my whispers for they are words of
comfort to reassure your heart.
Know that I'm internally yours;
Forever with you, always in my thoughts.
Just hold my hand and walk with me.

❧All of You❧

Relinquish to me you.
For I long for you at unawares.
In fact, your hold on me hurts so good.
My lonely for you flows down my cheeks in
private places.

For my longing for you is deep inside my being.
I hear your voice when only your thoughts
speak. Your touch comforts me through the
midget and the gentleman. They reassure my
hope. All is quelled and calm, and satisfied when
your smiling face appears.

Relinquish you to me.

⊰Counting Blessings⊱

I count it a blessing you're in my life, in my world, and in my existence.

I count it a joy when you encourage me when life has kicked my butt or my pain echoes loud and/or self-pity has set in.

I count it a privilege to know you beyond dreams, conversations and fantasy, Beloved.

I count it love when you touch me, kiss me or hold me.

I count it all love being an object of your affection and all the sincerity of heart.....
Thank you, Beloved.

❧You Can't Stop Love☙

Can't stop this thing we started.
With all your energies and all my charisma there
is no stopping us. We have a one-of-kind love.
Sincere hearts that meld together to conquer all
that is set before us.

We can't stop this thing we started.
Know that you bring out the very best in me and
you're my superstar on all levels. My tribute to
you is whatever your heart desires, and making
you smile when things seem bleak.

You and I can't stop this love thing we started.
It's bigger than both of us and I like it. Together
with God on our side, my Beloved, there's
nothing we cannot do.

We can't stop this thing we started, Mama Bear.

❧Does It Matter❧

Does it matter that I look into your eyes and see beautiful?

Does it matter that I see your smile and my heart melts?

Does it matter that my love for you holds no bounds.

The question I ask is from a place that you and you only have brought out of me.

Your quest to indulge in my world is granted by the sincerity of your soul.

You plan to love me forever and I plan to do the same.

My tears are of joys and the fact that you brought them forth only confirms that you loved me my heart from day one and I thank you for that.

I love you.

❦Because❧

Because you don't judge me.
Because you never stop being true to yourself or
to us.
Because you love me in your heart
unconditionally and sincerely.
Because you *Live Life Out Loud* and *On Purpose*.
Because you're more than beautiful to me.
Because of the many things you introduced me
too, I am that MAN to you.
Listen to me my heart, know that you're all I
ever want and need. Satisfied with us I am very
much.
Complete with you is what fills my prayers.
Because of all of the above and more plus you
believing in me is what makes my heart smile.
I love you Beloved with all my heart......

❧I Trust You❧

I place my heart in your hands because I can trust you to take care of it. You're allowed to gaze into my soul because your prayers are responsible for its healing. My mind is entrusted to you because within it you instill positive thoughts.

❧Anything for You❧

The kids are asleep. I lit candles for you to relax
too. Fresh linen is on the bed. Your favorite jazz
is playing low. I'm at your beck and call until
you fall asleep. What else would you like?

❧For All The Reasons❧

Yes, I do, for all the reasons you think not.
Yes, I will, because it's supposed to be this way.
Yes, I can, for you and you alone.
Yes, I am, for our children they deserve it as do you.
Yes. Yes. Yes.
It will be better.
You and I will make it.
It's my duty to take care of you. Us. We.

❧As of Lately❧

As of lately, I notice that I've disregarded you.
Unintentionally, but done just the same.
Asking for your forgiveness in my mind is NOT
enough.

Baby, if you allow me opportunities to do right
and make it up to you I won't let you down.
Smile and I'll know my kisses are on time.
Put your body into my hands where you know
you fit and I know it's alright to love you.

I know what fragrance you respect.
I know the fabric that makes you feel your best.
I know what duties to perform to relax you and
have your being good.

Because, I love you.
Because, you deserve this.
Because, I want to see you smile.
Just because and it's way overdue.

Lately, I noticed how beautiful you are....
Lately.

❧I'm Sorry❧

Just because I own what I did and take responsibility for my actions don't make it alright. It's you that I need but where do we go from here?

Loving you is never a question nor is it a thought. I'm more than good when you're by my side and with my heart shines.

All I'm asking you is to ponder your decision before you make it final. With all my heart and from your head to your feet I will always love you.

Baby I'm sorry....

❧To Be Forgiven❧

Beneath me you'll never be for more reason than
mentioned.
By my side always, because I need you,
In my head forever and a day for your voice is
my balance.
Keep me even when I seem distant and not
connected.
Pray for me when we haven't touched base.
love me because I'm still in your heart and that
matters.

Beloved, what you mean to me is beyond words
and often beyond my rationale and that's just
fine with me.

I need your smile and your laugh.
I need to feel when you roll your eyes at me
because I did it again.
I need to see your eyes that are so damn brown.
Forgiveness doesn't mean it's better.

Does it mean that I have chance to work my way
back through.
Allow me to see you and hold you and feel you
next to me.
Yes, Dear Baby, I'm begging—feeling
accomplished.

&I Want You Back&

My love for you has never lost its fire.
Although my kisses aren't what they once were.
Although my touch doesn't move you like it once
did.
My love for you will never die.....
What do I do Baby to get you back to me?
How do I get you back into my arms again?
Whom do I bribe? Where do I send the money?
I need you....

❧I Can't Let You Go❧

I can't let you go.
For reasons, more than my heart belongs to you,
I can't live without you.

I can't let you go.
For more reasons than there ain't no sunshine,
My smile is due to you.

I can't let you go;
Simply because, I love you;
Simply because I need you.

I can't let you go.
Because you're simply the best.
Because my world won't be the same;
Because only you have a hold on me.

For more than anything written,
I can't let you go.

❧I Want To Know❧

Would you date me again?
Would let me open the door for you, pull out
your chair, and stand up from sitting when you
arrive and when you are excused?
May I buy your flowers and your favorite
fragrance to get you to smile?

Would you date me again?
Would you let me take you to lunch on your
breaks at work?
Would you let me hold your hand as we walk
together through the park?
Would you date me after I made your family's
acquaintance and only the dog liked me?
May I slow dance with you sometime?

❧You Can't Make Me❧

I can't stop loving you.
I don't want to stop loving you.
You've made me a very happy man.
Would you please allow me to the opportunity to
make you smile again, and again?
Have whatever you want.
Have whatever you need.
I love you plain and simple, and every day.
I desire you more than not.
I can't stop loving you.
I don't want to stop loving you.
It's been a while since I've massaged your feet
and body or cooked you a good hot homemade
meal or taken you shopping.
It's overdue baby.
I can't stop loving you.
I don't want to stop loving you.
Have anything you want.
Have anything your heart desires.
I can't stop loving you.
I don't want to stop loving you.

❦I Supposed To Be❧

I'm supposed to be the one that loves you endlessly. You're the woman of my dreams and I refuse to let you go without a fight. It's my pleasure to be responsible for your wellbeing for the rest of our lives.

I'm the man you make love to without restrictions and limitations or any apprehension. You're my dream and fantasy come true.

Will you dance with me to the music of our heartbeats? Hold my hand and let me lead you as God leads me.

I'm supposed to be the one that loves you endlessly, for you are my everything.

⚞Delusions of You⚟

My mind is adrift with delusions of you.
While your presence is evident, I ask myself, do
you really exist?

The sounds of beauty and heat of your passion
and sweetness of your being I'm experiencing; I
will be chalking up as a figment of my
imagination.
Your eyes that usually have me entranced is not
there. The positive word from the soothing voice
that whispers I cannot hear.

Where are you?
Where have you gone?
Will you come back?
The heart that you loved with sincerity from a
far, misses you. Without your beautiful self-
occupying my world, I'm alone.

❧Allow Me❧

What do you mean I can't love you the way I know you like?
Why would you say no to my hands rubbing you down and them touching the spots that matter?
When did you decide that my lips, tongue and kisses to pleasure spots were no longer needed?
My desire is to please you when you need it most.
Allow me the privilege of soothe what aches on you.
Grant me the honor of giving you a relaxing touch.
May I make you smile by giving you kisses from head-to-toe and all over?
For when a sigh of relief comes from within you, I've done well by you.
Say yes to you fitting in my hands again.
Where can we do this? How do you want me to behave?
Know that I'm capable and won't let you down...promise.
May I?

⧼Do I Move You Still⧽

I was wondering.......
Does my touch still move you like it once did?
When I kiss your lips with mine, does it warm
you to your soul still?

Our heartbeats, do they still beat in unison
when you're in my arms? When I say, *I love you*
does it still give you butterflies in your navel?

Are You satisfied when I love you, with how love
you, and when and where I love you? When I
look into your eyes, do you know they are saying
you mean the absolute world to me, still?

ஃIf Only You Knew஭

If you only knew that, I'm sick without you.
Our Achilles heel, is the distance between us.
My body aches for your touch.
My heart yearns for your whispers.
My soul is sad without you near me.
All of me needs all of you in my world Beloved.
Another will never replace what I feel for you.
Another can't make me feel what I feel for you.
Beloved, I love you no matter what.
Beloved, I miss you plain and simple.
Beloved, I need you despite what surrounds me.
If only you knew how much I do want you.

Dear Baby,

The man you have fallen in love with is by no means complex. You know I am a lover of life, beautiful things, things learned and things taught. Most important my love is for the Lord Our God and his name Jesus (even though at times I don't act like it.)

In 45-years of living, I've learned a lot about me and I'm still learning. Mistakes have been made then and now still. Hearts have been broken mine and yours. Lots of tears have been shed yours and mine alike. You have been used and I have been too. It's safe to say that you and I have experienced what the world has to offer, good, bad, and the ugly. As I live and breathe, I'm reminded daily how a human I am and still look forward to tomorrow with you.

By now Baby, you know what makes me laugh, what upsets me, and what keeps me yours. You've given my children life, a great mother and an awesome woman to regard. You've become familiar with my taste for life and otherwise. I am ever so grateful for you being a positive motiving force in my life, for caring about me with no strings attached and for telling me the truth even if it hurts. I appreciate you, Beloved. The man you have fallen in love with is by no means complicated and with all that said, I love you.

Love Always,
Curty

Coming
Soon

Dear Baby: 2am
Baby You Sleep

By

Curtis Givens

www.ingramcontent.com/pod-product-compliance
Lightning Source LLC
Chambersburg PA
CBHW021027090426
42738CB00007B/928